D1200602

Images from

BITE

Gabrielle Mander

Bounty
BOOKS

Publisher: Polly Manguel

Editorial & Design Manager: Emma Hill

Designer: Ron Callow/Design 23, London

Production Manager: Neil Randles

First published in Great Britain in 2012
by Bounty Books,
a division of Octopus Publishing Group Ltd
Endeavour House,
189 Shaftesbury Avenue,
London WC2H 8JY
www.octopusbooks.co.uk

An Hachette UK Company
www.hachette.co.uk

ISBN: 978-0-753724-59-0

A CIP catalogue record for this book is available from the British Library

Printed and bound in China

The publisher wishes to thank all of the photographers (known and unknown) and the film distribution and
production companies whose images appear in this book. We apologize in advance for any omissions, or
neglect and will be pleased to make any corrections in future editions.

Introduction

It started, it would seem, not with a kiss, but with a bite. Ever since Eve took her first, tentative, disobedient nibble from that dratted apple, unleashing dangerous knowledge of good and evil, (with all that that implies), all hell broke loose and since that fateful moment, humankind has enjoyed a correspondingly ambiguous relationship with biting – and being bitten. In the wrong mouths – human or otherwise – teeth can become veritable weapons of mass destruction.

Many of our archetypal images, particularly those of beasts, monsters and other mythical creatures come to us through the imagination of artists and for over a century, moving pictures. These are the images we hold and share in our common consciousness. In recent times, CGI has presented a convincing way for us to realize our worst fears, although previously make-up and special effects were used to spectacular ends. So it is from cinema that the fabulous pictures in this book have been chosen. Since its earliest days, notable directors and great actors have mined the rich seam that is the pure terror of the 'bite'. This unique book takes a whistle stop tour of this hoard, in stunning and eclectic images and anecdotal and informative 'bite-sized' commentaries.

Take the deadly kiss of the broodingly handsome, Vitamin D deficient, (good/evil evil/good), but always irresistible vampire. They really don't exist, you know (someone had to say it), so we have to imagine them. The vampire has been an essential vision for the movie industry since 1921 and indeed, Bram Stoker's Count Dracula has featured in more films than any other fictional character, with over 170 appearances to date and his 'children of the night' have virtually taken over cinema screens in the 21st century, culminating in the Twilight saga.

Into every generation a vampire is born. In 1931, Bela Lugosi famously brought Count Dracula to life, in the eponymous movie of that year. Christopher Lee became synonymous with Dracula, when he donned the mantle from the late 1950s to the late 70s; indeed the tall, veteran actor was spotted quite recently, shopping in a fashionable London street, wearing a long black cloak and still looking every inch the Count, despite a plastic bag bearing the logo of a well-known supermarket. Regardless of stakes through the heart and exposure to sunlight, sons, daughters, houses and brides of Dracula proliferated during the 1960s and 70s. Dracula lives on. Francis Ford Coppola and Roman Polanski interpreted the vampire myths very differently and the world's first black, gay vampires appeared in 1972. Even Abbot and Costello got in on the act and another duo; Tom Cruise and Brad Pitt, hypnotized women everywhere with legendary lesbian vampires featured too, and, of course, the vampire hunters…

But what of other lethal bites from unimaginable creatures of frightening aspect? Steven Spielberg terrified the life out of audiences with the snapping jaws of the giant shark terrorizing bathers in a quiet seaside resort and man-eating dinosaurs from a long forgotten prehistoric island, bite for their lives against the World War I mariners unfortunate enough to be shipwrecked there. Modern day fears of the consequences of man's interference with nature are graphically displayed in the unusual *Black Sheep* (2006) exploring the possibility of genetically modified lambs turned 'weresheep' devouring their shepherds. Dinosaurs feature quite regularly in the stories told around the log burning effect fire in our own time. Perhaps we need to reassure ourselves that their extinction and our survival is not accidental?

Gnashing the teeth that God, or evolution, gave most creatures and some plants, (it would seem), in creative and mostly lethal ways is a regular occurrence in nightmares and when it comes to man's inhumanity to man, we are unsurpassed; think cannibalism, and very unethical dentistry. Indeed any analysis of the history of 20th and 21st century iconography would appear to suggest that we have collective and all-consuming Odontophobia!

Bite is a celebration of all things toothsome, from apples to zombies with a side order of good old-fashioned gluttony and a little gentle nibbling to go.

It started with a bite...

Polly Moran, Jimmy Durante: *Hollywood Party*, 1934
Director: Richard Boleslavski, MGM

Our hero, D'Leh, faced with a fairly disgruntled sabre-tooth tiger, needs courage, calm, skill and strength. Creating a convincing image for the cat required the visual effects team to achieve some of the most difficult elements of their craft; 'wet', 'wet fur', 'water' and 'creature animation'.

Steven Strait: *10,000 Years BC*, 2008
Director: Roland Emmerich, Warner Bros.

9

Why do bad things happen to good people? The well-intentioned Dr Susan McCallister, with help from Carter Blake, shown here, are looking for a cure for Alzheimer's disease in an isolated research facility, when they become the guinea pigs for a trio of intelligent sharks!

Thomas Jane: *Deep Blue Sea*, 1999
Director: Renny Harlin, Warner Bros.

Fearless National Geographic film crew member, Warren Westridge comes face to face with fear, and the world's largest and deadliest snake, when a mad hunter carries the team along on his lunatic quest to find the Anaconda.

Jonathan Hyde: *Anaconda*, 1997
Director: Luis Llosa, Columbia

It's an open and shut case for Ace Ventura, pet detective, as he grapples with a very large crocodile, encountered in his search for a rare, white bat, the symbol of an African tribe. He is more than a match for the croc in the flashing white teeth department.

Jim Carrey: *Ace Ventura: When Nature Calls*, 1995
Director: Steve Oedekerk, Morgan Creek

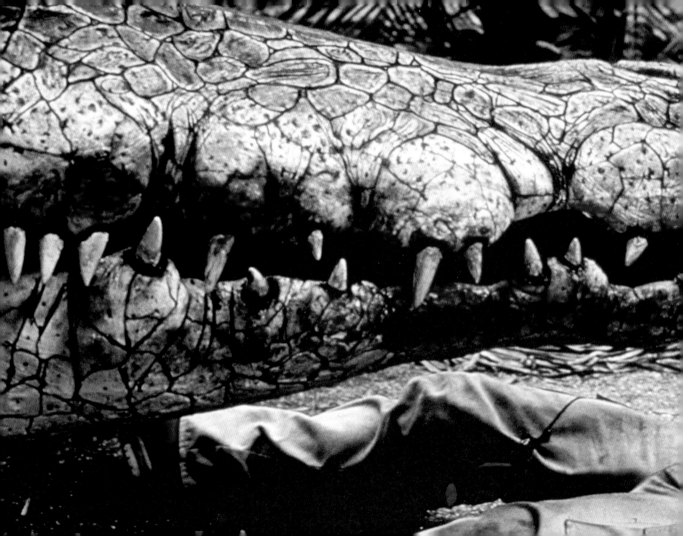

Just when you thought it was safe to crash a hijacked plane into a Mexican swamp, giant crocodiles appear from the slimy depths. Proof, if proof were required, that crime doesn't pay. As ever, it is the innocent who suffer, the survivors are driven on by the robbers and menaced at every step.

Chuck Walczak: *Crocodile 2: Death Swamp*, 2001
Director: Gary Jones, Nu Image Films
Photo: Syamal Rao

"We're going to need a bigger boat" says Sheriff Martin Brody (left), with masterly understatement, when faced for the first time with a Great White Shark amongst the splashing children and weekend sailors in the previously peaceful waters of the tiny seaside resort of Amity. A Spielberg classic.

Roy Scheider: *Jaws*, 1975
Director: Steven Spielberg, Universal

"Something you wouldn't dare to imagine is alive," hissed the poster for this preacher versus the devil picture (right). Also known as King Cobra, here we find Satan, like Lord Voldemort, embodied in the form of a huge snake. Will our hero's Druidic ancestry help or hinder in the battle to come?

Jaws of Satan, 1982
Director: Bob Claver, United Artists

This title speaks for itself. Giant prehistoric creatures battle it out for supremacy of the sea off the coast of California. It seems they really cannot help destroying vital infrastructure like the Golden Gate Bridge, as they go about the grisly business of mutual destruction. It's a size thing.

Mega Shark Vs. Giant Octopus, 2009
Director: Jack Perez, Giant Seafood

" *Half-Shark.*
Half-Octopus.
All Terror "

A giant octopus is something to contend with. A massive shark should be avoided. When a military genius combines the two, to make the mighty sharktopus, there is mayhem waiting to happen. As a 'responsible' scientist he now has to destroy his own creation. Has he never heard of Frankenstein?

Sharktopus, 2010
Director: Declan O'Brien, Syfy Pictures Original Film

The mutant shark strikes again! This time, a cave with a school of six mutant Great Whites is found in South Africa. One has already been captured and installed in the Water World Park. Only Samantha, Nick and shark hunter Roy, from the Discovery Channel, (what would they do without him?) stand between Cape Town and disaster.

Shark Attack 2, 2000
Director: David Worth, Nu Image Films

Here, Jessica Szohr, as herself, experiences the terror of a school of deadly piranha heading for her face, with a determined look in their eyes and their mouths wide open. It is hard to believe that flesh-nibbling fish are extremely popular in beauty salons, just to provide smooth feet. Do we really have to suffer to be beautiful?

Jessica Szohr: *Piranha 3D*, 2010
Director: Alexandre Aja, Weinstein Co.

Unwanted baby alligator plus unwanted growth hormone-eating lab rats together equal an urban myth and universal terror realized: a giant alligator emerging from the Chicago sewers (left) to terrorize the city. This particular 'gator was normal-sized, filmed in a miniature set, as the giant mechanical model had a diva moment.

Alligator, 1980
Director: Lewis Teague, Alligator Inc.

"Fang and claw killers stalk the city streets!" read the tagline on the poster for this film (below). The carnage shown here is the result of animal cult membership and murderous intent. The beautifully trained big cats lent style and authenticity to the plot, in which a zoo owner is able to indulge his worst fantasies.

Black Zoo, 1963
Director: Robert Gordon, Allied Artists

When greed and mischance collide with nature, an environmental disaster movie is sure to follow. Here, a hapless investor is shown in a life and death struggle with a 'weresheep'; the result of an ill-conceived experiment in genetic engineering on a sprawling New Zealand farm. The bloodthirsty wolves in sheep's clothing create mayhem, even attacking Jonathan King in a Hitchcock-style cameo role.

Jono Manks: *Black Sheep* 2006
Director: Jonathan King, Live Stock Films
Photo: Ken George

" Man's best friend is now man's worst fiend. ,,

As if the most enduring blood-sucking vampire in fiction were not enough of a horror, an inadvertent unearthing of a tomb in Romania resurrects Zoltan, hound of Dracula. This classic 70's flick features 'Drake', as the Count's modern descendent, who contemplates litigation against the makers of Dracula movies, for the use of his name.

Zoltan...Hound of Dracula, 1978
Director: Albert Band, Hammer

What is the answer to nerdy florist Seymour's prayers? Something on which to exercise his horticultural skills, which he can name after love interest Audrey and to which he can feed both his rival for her affections and his nagging boss. What better than a large flesh-eating plant?

Rick Moranis: *Little Shop of Horrors*, 1986
Director: Frank Oz , Warner Bros.

"Cowboys Battle Monsters in the Lost World of the Forbidden Valley"

Every show is looking for a jaw-dropping act to bring in the crowds and Wild West attractions, circa 1900, are no exception. These show folks have set their hearts on a fabled dinosaur that dwells in a forbidden valley. An expedition (featuring the obligatory aristocratic British paleontologist) is formed and the fast-paced action and Harryhausen's terrific special effects that follow are no surprise, though nonetheless enjoyable for that.

The *Valley of Gwangi*, 1969
Director: Jim O'Connolly, Warner Bros.

"Size does matter". As if growth hormone-mutated crocodiles in Chicago sewers were not enough, Manhattan is menaced by a radioactively mutated, giant lizard named Godzilla (left). In this remake of the Japanese original, his rampage was financed by a mega budget. At last, this shot explains why you can never get a cab to go over the river.

Godzilla, 1998
Director: Roland Emmerich, Columbia

If New York's Empire State Building was no match for King Kong, what are the odds of London's Big Ben (right) withstanding the onslaught of the mighty Gorgo and why do these unnaturally large animals take such enraged exception to our national monuments? It's the scale of the destruction that is so disturbing.

Gorgo, 1960
Director: Eugene Lourie, King Brothers Productions

*" **Right place, wrong time.** "*

Dr Rick Marshall and his research team give a whole new meaning to straphanging, when they are sucked into a space/time vortex. Encountering all manner of prehistoric and fantastic creatures, none of them friendly, their only ally is a primate named Chaka.

Anna Friel, Danny McBride, Will Ferrell: *Land of the Lost,* 2009
Director: Brad Silberling, Universal/Mosaic/Relativity

Dr Grant had vowed never to return to the islands after that dinosaur unpleasantness in Jurassic Park and yet…The result might have been foreseen – you can't put the dinosaur back in the bottle. Incidentally, the Spinosaurus was the largest animatronic ever built, weighing 12 tons and operated by hydraulics and the effects crew used 250 gallons of oatmeal to represent Spinosaur droppings.

Michael Jeter, Alessandro Nivola, Tea Leoni, Sam Neill, William H. Macy:
Jurassic Park III, 2001
Director: Joe Johnston, Amblin/Universal

These giant, man-eating crocodiles seem to turn up in the most unlikely places. This time, the calm waters of Lake Placid are disturbed by a huge carnivore and, as is so often the case, it is the very expensive equipment that gets destroyed. Yes, it's all fun and games until someone gets their helicopter eaten.

Lake Placid, 1999
Director: Steve Miner, Phoenix Pictures

Will movie scientists never learn that releasing the DNA of pre-historic creatures, some with very, very sharp teeth and others of great size is just not a good idea? It might also be a mistake to then open a dinosaur theme park (left), even if it is on an island. Although the motor industry might benefit – that truck will need to be replaced and insurance probably won't cover it.

Jurassic Park, 1993
Director: Steven Spielberg, Amblin/Universal

"It's not WHERE they are, it's WHEN", ran the line on the poster advertising this movie (right). A World War I German U-boat sinks a British ship and takes the survivors on board. Lost at sea, the submarine carries them to the unknown island of Caprona, where they are attacked by man-eating dinosaurs and fail to make friends with the native Neanderthals. Before CGI, the low budget special effects were just as scary to 1970s audiences.

The Land That Time Forgot, 1974
Director: Kevin Connor, Amicus

47

The *Nightmare on Elm Street* films are surely some of the most frightening ever screened and undead serial killer, Freddie Krueger, one of the most creatively fiendish characters to emerge in this genre. In this incarnation he finds a way to torture the survivors of his previous spree, in their dreams. They must master 'lucid dreaming' to survive. Is nowhere safe?

Patricia Arquette: *A Nightmare on Elm Street 3: Dream Warriors*, 1987
Director: Chuck Russell, New Line

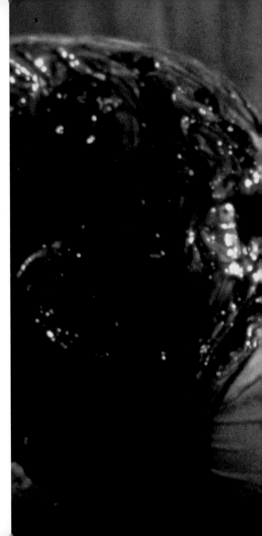

> ❝ *We Have Witnessed The Beginning...*
> *We Have Seen The Apocalypse...*
> *Now We Face Extinction...* ❞

This, the third in the *Resident Evil* series, finds Alice fighting not only the evil Umbrella Corporation, but also a veritable ark of hideously terrifying creatures with malevolent intent, including killer crows and flesh-eating zombies. That deadly T-virus has a lot to answer for.

Resident Evil: Extinction, 2007
Director: Russell Mulcahy, Constantin Film/Davis-Films

*"...No details. No witnesses.
No evidence. Until now.*

When a news crew is quarantined inside a building in Los Angeles, with no contact with the outside world, it is for them to chronicle the unthinkable events surrounding a virus that turns decent citizens into flesh-devouring monsters. It would seem that James McCreedy will not be available for comment.

Andrew Fiscella: *Quarantine*, 2008
Director: John Erick Dowdle, Andale Pictures

The original, and some would say, the best. This film marks the legendary first Hollywood appearance of Count Dracula (left), a vampire with elegance, if not verve. Interestingly, the trademark fangs did not appear in this movie and it had no real musical soundtrack to lend menace. Producers believed that such a recent innovation would be unacceptable to audiences in scenes where no music would play in real life. Universal Studios commissioned a new musical score from composer Philip Glass, which premiered at The Brooklyn Academy of Music in 1999.

Frances Dade, Bela Lugosi: *Dracula*, 1931
Director: Tod Browning, Universal

By the turn of the Millennium, cinema's Count Dracula had been vanquished and resurrected over 100 times, but in this incarnation (right), freed inadvertently by thieves, he travels to New Orleans to find Mary, the daughter of his arch-nemesis, Van Helsing. Handsome Gerard Butler adds to the legend of the irresistible vampire, although in this scene it would seem to be a case of the biter, bit.

Jeri Ryan: *Dracula*, 2000
Director: Patrick Lussier, Wes Craven Film
Photo: Ron Phillips

Also known as *Andy Warhol's Dracula*, this shoestring budget film was shot on location in Italy. Nearby, Roman Polanski was filming *What?* and was persuaded to give a cameo performance in *Blood for Dracula*. Evidently, he was pressed for time, as he wears the same moustache in both movies. Kier's performance must count as one of the campest Draculas in a long history of inherent campness. But his quest for the blood of 'wirgins' provides an entertaining plot twist in the permissive seventies.

Udo Kier: *Blood For Dracula*, 1974
Director: Paul Morrissey, CCC

Grief stricken, Stella Oleson has travelled the world trying to convince others that she did not imagine the vampire clan, which killed her husband in an Alaskan siege. Here (left), vampire, Jennifer feasting upon her kill, looks pretty convincingly real, but will she prevail against the revenge of Stella and a group of like-minded survivors?

Katie Keating: *30 Days of Night: Dark Days*, 2010
Director: Ben Ketai, Dark Horse Entertainment

"Every Family Has its Demons", shouted the tagline for this movie and after two centuries of ruin, the dysfunctional descendants of *pater familias* vampire Barnabus Collins, illustrate this fact admirably (right). Veteran vampire, Christopher Lee makes an appearance to add gravitas to proceedings.

Johnny Depp: *Dark Shadows*, 2012
Director: Tim Burton, Warner Bros.

"Waitress: [to Mamuwalde]
Hi! What'll you have?
Mamuwalde:
Make it a Bloody Mary."

As the almost inevitable consequence of getting the decorators in, unwitting interior designers buy an ancient coffin and ship it to Los Angeles, unaware that it is the far-from-final resting place of African prince, Mamuwalde. Mamuwalde and his wife Tuva had dined with Dracula at Castle Dracula, in Transylvania in 1870, but alas when he said he would like to have them for dinner, he wasn't joking. Mamuwalde resisted the Count's blandishments and is cursed, henceforth, to be known as Blacula: shown here claiming his latest victim.

William Marshall: *Blacula*, 1972
Director: William Crain, AIP

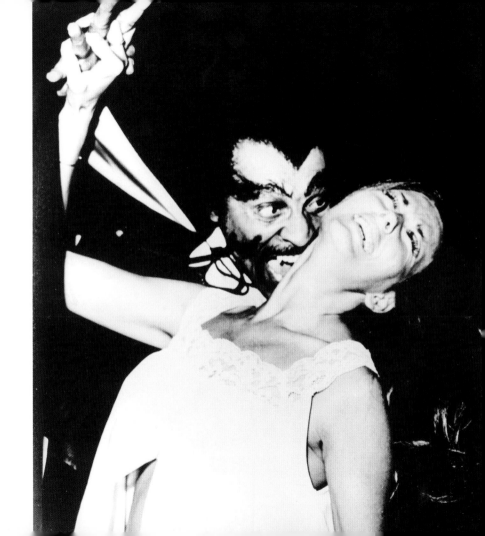

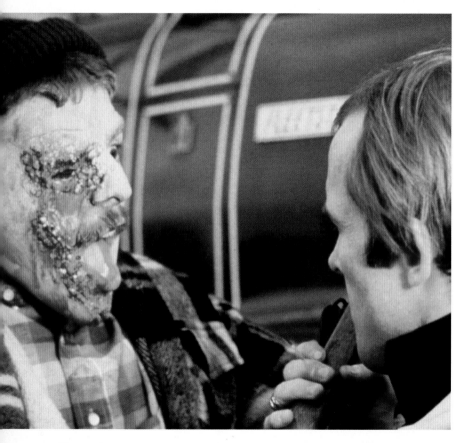

"When there's no more room in hell, the dead will walk the earth…" and possibly hang out at the mall and pick up a snack. Two SWAT team members, a traffic reporter and his television executive girlfriend are holed up in this particular deserted Philadelphia shopping mall, trying to avoid becoming hamburger for a plague of Zombies, in this sequel (left) to the classic horror, *Night of the Living Dead*.

Scott Reiniger: *Dawn of the Dead*, 1978
Director: George A. Romero, Laurel Group

A group of male-bonding pals take a trip to a remote village to help Vince come to terms with his divorce. The perfidy of women must have been on the writer's mind as they discover that all the women have contracted a virus, turning them into man-hating cannibals. Here (right), Neil discovers one of the pitfalls of attracting female attention.

Danny Dyer: *Doghouse*, 2009
Director: Jake West, Carnaby Film Productions

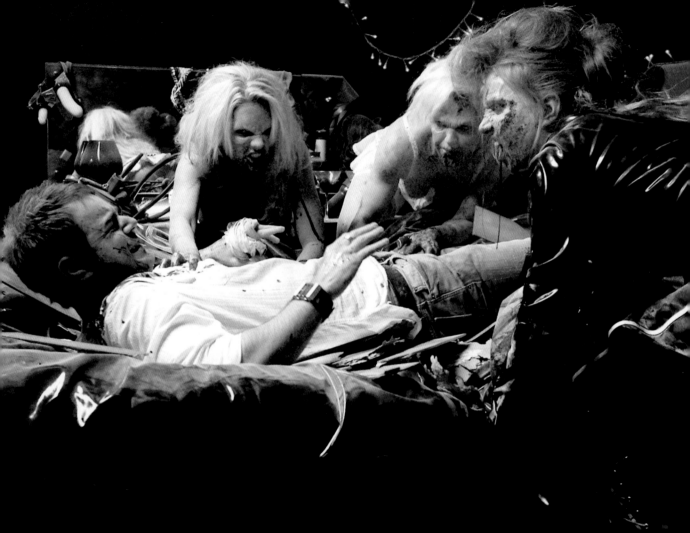

Once upon a time there was only one vampire who counted – Dracula – and it seems that he is still the man when 21st century vamps need a leader. Danica, shown here, is one of the four who have resurrected Dracula, and Blade is the freelance, lone hero vampire hunter wanted by the FBI, who must join forces with the Nightstalkers to face his most challenging enemy yet.

Parker Posey: *Blade: Trinity*, 2004
Director: David S. Goyer, New Line
Photo: Diyah Pera

> **HANNIBAL KING:**
> *[to Danica, as she is dying from the Daystar Plague]*
> *Hang in there, kitten. I'll get help.*

"Love Never Dies" proclaimed one of the taglines to this movie. Faithful to the author's original text, in perhaps the first serious treatment of the subject, Coppola's film is based on the classic love triangle of one woman, one man and one vampire. Inspired by a visiting young lawyer's love for his English fiancée, Mina, Dracula imprisons Harker (shown here suffering at the fangs of Dracula's vampire temptresses) in his castle and goes to England in search of love.

Keanu Reeves, Monica Bellucci: *Bram Stoker's Dracula*, 1992
Director: Francis Ford Coppola, Zoetrope/Columbia

Baron Meinster is a son only a mother could love! He has vampiric designs on the lovely Marianne and the ladies of her exclusive school. Once the scion of a noble house, as his mother recognizes, he is not what he once was. Fortunately, Van Helsing, vampire hunter and vanquisher of Dracula, is on his way.

David Peel: *Brides of Dracula*, 1960 Director: Terence Fisher, Hammer

"*MARIANNE DANIELLE:*
[gasping in disbelief]
Then that poor prisoner, in the tower.
He is your son?
BARONESS MEINSTER:
He was my son. Now he is only...
a beast of the night."

> ## " *The Time: Now.*
> ## *The Place: Kings Road, Chelsea.*
> ## *The Killer: Count Dracula.* "

This tagline took full advantage of the backdrop of swinging London, for a film that offered a new slant on the Dracula legend. In a present day setting we watch the descendants of Van Helsing at the mercy of the vengeful Count; with lovely Stephanie Beecham as Jessica Van Helsing and Christopher Lee as a peerless Dracula.

Caroline Munro, Christopher Lee: *Dracula AD, 1972*
Director: Alan Gibson, Hammer

Synchronicity between life and life on the silver screen, leads student filmmakers spoofing a zombie-pic, to end by producing a real-life documentary, chronicling real dead men walking. The late Mrs. Moynihan (left), departs radically from food hygiene in the kitchen, and that meat-free diet.

Trish Adams: *Diary of the Dead*, 2007
Director: George A. Romero, Artfire Films/
Romero-Grunwald

PC Erny (right) seems to have succumbed to the lure of the lair of the white worm, although this on-the-spot fine appears disproportionate. After all, playing the bagpipes isn't a crime – or is it? Hugh Grant also appeared, unusually cast as Lord James D'Ampton.

Paul Brooke: *The Lair of the White Worm*, 1988
Director: Ken Russell, White Lair/Vestron

"Sleep all day. Party all night. Never grow old. Never die. It's fun to be a vampire." It may take a while for the parents of teenage boys to recognize the symptoms of vampirism, if these are the official guidelines, as the first two seem to be par for the course. David's fangs (left) would seem to be a bit of a giveaway.

Kiefer Sutherland: *The Lost Boys*, 1987
Director: Joel Schumacher, Warner Bros.

" *MAX:*
It was all going to be so perfect, Lucy.
Just like one big, happy family.
Your boys...and my boys.
EDGAR FROG:
Great! The Bloodsucking
Brady Bunch! *"*

Klaus Kinski's distinctive appearance in this movie resulted (allegedly) from the star's reluctance to spend hours in make-up, in order to recreate the original Werner Herzog/Nosferatu look. Oddly, it enhances the quality of introspective, undead angst that pervades this 'serious' vampire picture. Venice, with its timeless and decaying splendour is the perfect context for the plot.

Klaus Kinski: *Vampire in Venice (Nosferatu a Venezia)*, 1988
Director: Augusto Caminito, Scena Film

The poster for this zombie picture warned audiences to "Kiss your nerves goodbye". The lone survivor of a zombie attack and the strangers holed up with him in a remote cabin risk kissing their limbs goodbye, as the flesh-eaters rally. The hideous teeth with which these zombies are endowed signal poor dental hygiene, and their intentions, pretty clearly.

Evil Dead II, 1987
Director: Sam Raimi, DEG/Renaissance

A nineteenth-century female vampire is hired in the twentieth to assassinate prominent members of 'the Illuminati' an elite business community. Pursued by Scotland Yard, and the Illuminati, she must fight to survive; one bloodsucker versus many, some might say.

Christopher Adamson: *Razor Blade Smile*, 1998
Director: Jake West, Palm Pictures

Based on the best-selling novel by Anne Rice, this story of the loves, loss and loneliness of the Vampire Lestat and his corruption of Brad Pitt excited female audiences all over the world. The joint attentions of vampires Tom Cruise and Brad Pitt would have undoubtedly set this girl's pulse racing, had she still had a pulse to race. Ah, love and death – the big questions!

Tom Cruise, Brad Pitt, Belina Logan: *Interview with the Vampire*, 1994
Director: Neil Jordan, Geffen Pictures
Photo: François Duhamel

81

"Who says Vampires are no laughing matter?" declared Roman Polanski (left), who plays it for laughs, attacking the genre with brio, and the plot with gusto. Set in Transylvania and shot on location in Italy, the script has all the ingredients of a good vamp flick; batty professor, naïve, lovelorn assistant, lovely innkeeper's daughter and Count Krolock – the lustful, undead villain of aristocratic mien.

Iain Quarrier, Roman Polanski:
The Fearless Vampire Killers, 1967
Director: Roman Polanski,
Cadre Films/Filmways Pictures

No hypnotic trance and dulcet Transylvanian tones preceded this kiss. Dr Ravna (right) is unfortunate enough to be bitten by the "Giant devil Bats... summoned from the caves of Hell to destroy the lust of the Vampires" as the tagline tells us.

Kiss of the Vampire, 1962
Director: Don Sharp, Hammer

Queen Carmilla, ruler of the lesbian vampire killers feasting on human flesh. She holds the womenfolk of a rural town in thrall, thanks to one of those ancient curses. The menfolk seem unable to come up with a solution other than to sacrifice two unfortunate young lads, by sending them out onto the moor. It seems those team-building exercises were a waste of money.

Silvia Filatova, Myanna Buring: *Lesbian Vampire Killers*, 2009
Director: Phil Claydon, Alliance Films/Momentum

Some scientists will do anything for love, including devising a dubious treatment to restore the appearance of a beautiful woman, horribly disfigured in an accident. This beastly botox requires frequent top-ups and the scientist's source of flesh blood owes much to his monstrous metamorphosis (left).

Susanne Loret, Alberto Lupo: *Atom Age Vampire (Seddok, l'erede di Satana)*, 1960
Director: Anton Giulio Majano, Leone Film

Does television adversely influence the young? Peter Vincent, venal host of TV's *Fright Night*, suspends his disbelief in the supernatural to help (with the aid of a cash bonus) young fan, Charlie, expose and vanquish the vampires next door (right).

Amanda Bearse: *Fright Night*, 1985
Director: Tom Holland, Columbia

Writers of horror stories should be very careful when accepting invitations from sinister old gentlemen. Vincent Price (right), host of 'the monster club', reveals his true identity and it is more frightening than any fiction our hapless author could imagine.

John Carradine, Vincent Price: *The Monster Club*, 1980
Director: Roy Ward Baker, ITV Global

This mash-up of classic horror film characters finds Frankenstein's monster, a werewolf and Mr. Hyde, not to mention more than one bride of the polygamous Dracula, in cahoots and under attack from the "one name they all fear" Van Helsing. No, not Abraham, but his less famous younger brother Gabriel. Incidentally, the 'Bram', in Bram Stoker, author of *Dracula*, is short for Abraham.

Richard Roxburgh: *Van Helsing*, 2004
Director: Stephen Sommers, Universal

It seems sometimes that the frightening modern world, filtered through a camera lens and writers' imaginations, is overrun by mythical monsters: 'supernature', as it were, 'red in tooth and claw'. In the mid-20th century, filmmakers represented civilization under threat by sci-fi aliens. This classy 21st century TV series finds the individual and his family terrorized by a plague of zombies.

Walking Dead, 2010, AMC-TV

93

The ultimate urbane English gentleman, David Niven, turns tour guide to lure victims to his castle. The ageing vampire, in need of fresh blood to resurrect his lost love, Vampira, accidently morphs into a black woman. Surreal and lighthearted, this picture was released as *Old Dracula* in the USA, in response to the success of *Young Frankenstein*.

Veronica Carlson, David Niven: *Vampira*, 1973
Director: Clive Donner, World Film Services/AIP

This is no idle threat from the violent undead, in this classic 70's zombie drama, banned for excessive gore in several countries. Will the doctor desperately seeking a cure for an epidemic of flesh-eating find the formula in time? The trouble with the selfish undead is that they have no interest in being helped to their eternal rest. All they think about is where their next meal is coming from.

Zombie Flesh Eaters, 1979
Director: Lucio Fulci, Variety Film

" *We are going to eat you* "

In 1968, the dead walked amongst us, in one of the scariest zombie films ever made. The not so recently departed, bear down inexorably on the living, locked inside a remote farmhouse. In this update of the classic, the living dead walk off the screen and into our nightmares with 3D gore and terror in every heavy footstep.

Joshua Desrochas: *Night of the Living Dead 3D*, 2006
Director: Jeff Broadstreet, Lux Digital

" *Making a meal of it.* "

This is probably the best-known example of 'making a meal of it' in cinema history. The hungry little tramp, and consummate master of comedy, dines on an old boot as if it were a gourmet feast, with a unique combination of pathos and humour.

Charlie Chaplin: *The Gold Rush*, 1925
Director: Charlie Chaplin, United Artists

A growing boy needs his food, but if DJ Johnson is going to grow up, rather than out, he might want to start 'portion control' now. Will this chaotic family make it to Missouri and a family reunion in this comedy road movie? It might depend on how many pit stops they have to make.

Solange Knowles, Lil Bow Wow: *Johnson Family Vacation*, 2004
Director: Christopher Erskin, Fox Searchlight

Spirited heroine Carmen (left) seems to be taking exception to, and a bite out of, heart-throb hero Joe. Perhaps being tied up has something to do with it? This production of Bizet's *Carmen* was a great success on the Broadway stage and the film was box office gold. Although Belafonte and Dandridge were both accomplished singers, neither had the training, or the range, to sing operatic roles. Their singing voices were dubbed, by LeVern Hutcherson and Marilyn Horne, respectively.

Harry Belafonte, Dorothy Dandridge: *Carmen Jones*, 1954
Director: Otto Preminger, 20th Century Fox

Holly Golightly (right), Truman Capote's naïvely loveable good-time girl, returns home in the early hours, taking a bite of her 'breakfast' croissant, whilst feasting her eyes on the windows of the legendary jewellers Tiffany, in New York. Holly's oversized sunglasses, little black dress and long, black evening gloves epitomized a look that millions of women have tried to emulate since. It is said that Capote originally wanted Marilyn Monroe for the part. Fortunately, she was busy. It is now impossible to imagine anyone other than the inimitable Audrey as Holly.

Audrey Hepburn: *Breakfast At Tiffany's*, 1961
Director: Blake Edwards, Paramount

A seafood platter presents limitless challenges to Rowan Atkinson's brilliant creation, the naïve and hapless Mr. Bean. Socially difficult seafood ranks with which knife and fork to use at a formal banquet as most people's worst nightmare, but Mr. Bean turns hell into a holiday and farce into an art form.

Rowan Atkinson: *Mr. Bean's Holiday,* 2007
Director: Steve Bendelack, Universal/Working Title

Do we believe that horizontal stripes are flattering to the fuller figure? Poor Augustus Gloop, doomed to obesity by gluttony, his name, his mother (naturally), wardrobe, and his creator, author Roald Dahl. Augustus is one of a cast of greedy, selfish, or spoilt children whose misbehaviour forms a striking contrast to poor boy Charlie's virtue. Augustus is shown here eating the set, putting himself out of the running for the big prize.

Philip Wiegratz: *Charlie and the Chocolate Factory*, 2005
Director: Tim Burton, Warner Bros.
Photo: Peter Mountain

Teenager Lita Hazlett (left) attempts to reconcile her warring parents in this long-forgotten movie. It is hard to see how providing an all-you-can-eat marshmallow buffet for the male chorus line would help, but the past is a foreign country. Betty Bronson's successful career included forty films, before her final performance in *Evil Knievel* (1971).

Betty Bronson, Adolphe Menjou:
Are Parents People?, 1925
Director: Malcolm St Clair, Paramount

There is a fine line between a nibble and a nip, as self-appointed 'Count' Karanzim (right), the Russian émigré gigolo will tell you. Overzealous nibbling could scare the lady off before she is relieved of cash and jewels. Biting the hand that feeds you is not to be recommended.

Erich Von Stroheim, Mae Busch: *Foolish Wives*, 1922
Director: Erich Von Stroheim, Universal

Beethoven brings something special
to the table and gives new meaning to
the term 'binge eating' in this stolen
puppies, cute kid caper, with the very
appealing, if unwittingly destructive
St Bernard.

Charles Grodin: *Beethoven's 2nd*, 1993
Director: Rod Daniel, Universal
Photo: Christine Loss

Fish on the bone can present certain challenges to the uninitiated. Rarely, however, does it engender such a response of bemusement and horror as here, unless it shows some indication that it intends to bite back.

Tom Green: *Freddy Got Fingered*, 2001
Director: Tom Green, New Regency
Photo: Chris Helcermanas-Benge

The path to a bogus insurance claim never did run smooth. Harry Hinkle (left), sports cameraman is beginning to regret allowing his crooked lawyer brother-in-law to persuade him into the scam, initiated after he was accidentally hit by a football player when filming the game. A future cash payment isn't worth much when you can't even touch the tempting food in front of you, let alone get your teeth into it.

Jack Lemmon: *The Fortune Cookie*, 1966
Director: Billy Wilder, United Artists

Victor Frankenstein is the archetypal mad scientist: arrogant, driven, without conscience. Determined to create a human being from unmatched spare body parts (he probably wears odd socks too), he is not particular about their provenance (the parts not the socks). Of course, the result is a horror beyond imagining. Here the unfortunate monster, played by David Prowse, the future Darth Vader, gets to grips with the concept of lunch (right).

David Prowse: *The Horror of Frankenstein*, 1970
Director: Jimmy Sangster, Hammer

Is the food you eat damaging your health? This documentary takes a serious look at the fast food industry, and how corporate interests may undermine the health and wellbeing of consumers and providers alike. This picture could be taken on any day, in any city, in the western world. Is it time to keep our minds open and our mouths shut?

Food, Inc., 2008
Director: Robert Kenner, Magnolia Pictures

> **LT. FRANK DREBIN:** *Now, Jane, what can you tell us about the man you saw last night?*
> **JANE SPENCER:** *He's Caucasian.*
> **ED HOCKEN:** *Caucasian?*
> **JANE SPENCER:** *Yeah, you know, a white guy. A moustache. About six-foot-three.*
> **LT. FRANK DREBIN:** *Awfully big moustache.*

Never underestimate the comedic value of a lobster; they so often bite back in one way or another. Here we see the unexpected pitfalls of being seated next to Lieutenant Drebin whilst he addresses a large crustacean.

Leslie Nielsen: The *Naked Gun 2½: The Smell Of Fear*, 1991
Director: David Zucker, Paramount
Photo: Ron Phillips

> *"These Addams men, where do you find them?*
> **MORTICIA:**
> *It has to be damp."*

Horror meets high comedy when the gothic Addams family attempts to rescue Uncle Fester from a golddigger. Here, the romantic Gomez displays both his dazzling knife throwing and catching skills, whilst dancing a mean tango and flashing his maniacal winning smile.

Raul Julia: *Addams Family Values*, 1993
Director: Barry Sonnenfeld, Paramount
Photo: Melinda Sue Gordon

Sushi – the fast food of the 21st century. The smart money is on healthy, fresh food, with as little cooking as possible. Bite-sized morsels of omega rich, tempting delicacies from Japanese cuisine tease the palate, satisfy the eye and nourish the body. There is hardly anything for the teeth to do!

The Full Picture, 2008
Director: Jon Bowden, One Big Head Films

125

As an antidote to ennui and disillusionment, hiring a group of prostitutes, escaping to the country and vowing to eat yourselves to death smacks a little of overkill (left). But, each to his own.

Andrea Ferreol, Philippe Noiret: *Blow Out*
(La Grande Bouffe), 1973
Director: Marco Ferreri, Mara Films/Films 66

Dr Julia Harris has evidently not read the manual on inappropriate behavior in the workplace, as she blatantly nibbles Dale's ear (right). In a neat role reversal, she is one of three horrible bosses marked down, with the willing aid of disgruntled employees, for demotion – six feet under.

Charlie Day, Jennifer Aniston: *Horrible Bosses*, 2011
Director: Seth Gordon, New Line

Ronnie O'Dowd – seen here (left) having her finger bitten, escapes her domestic problems by going in search of her father in New York. She finds him, new problems, some friendship, a romance, and an unexpected career as a pro-boxer. *Variety* described the movie as "Thelma and Louise meets Rocky".

Margi Clarke: *Blonde Fist*, 1991
Director: Frank Clarke, Blue Dolphin/Film 4

Third-class alien Giles (right), bobbing for apples? In this tongue-in-cheek horror movie, aliens replace the missing population of a small town and hunt down human flesh to stock their intergalactic fast-food chain. Coming soon to a town near you.

Craig Smith: *Bad Taste*, 1987
Director: Peter Jackson, Wingnut Films

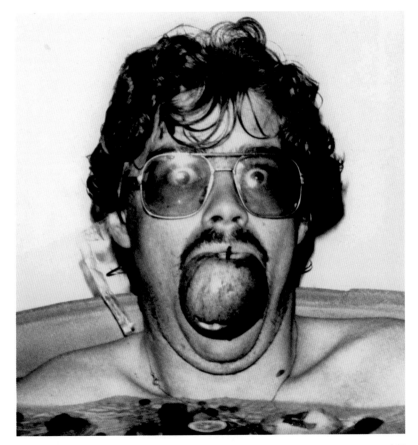

129

At this very minute there will be an episode of *I Love Lucy* (left) showing somewhere in the world. The lasting appeal of this 1950s comedy show is only matched by the enduring power of Lucy herself and, judging by this shot, the strength of her bite!

William Frawley, Desi Arnaz, Lucille Ball: *I Love Lucy*
1951-1957, CBS-TV

This Stooges' wartime parody of Hitler (right) uses a feast to emphasize the greed of the fascist dictator, when most of Europe was preparing for famine. During filming, Moe was late for his daughter's birthday party, so to the surprise of friends and neighbours, he spent the entire party dressed as Hitler, stopping traffic and causing numerous calls to the police.

The Three Stooges: *I'll Never Heil Again*, 1941
Director: Jules White, Columbia

"Is he crazy?...or is he light years ahead of us?" This was the tagline that intrigued and teased audiences, almost as much as the movie itself. But the greatest mystery remains, what exactly is the mental patient/alien Prot (to rhyme with goat) eating (left)?

Kevin Spacey: *K-Pax*, 2001
Director: Iain Softley, IMF/Intermedia Films/Pathé

An out-of-the-way diner becomes the unlikely battleground for the survival of the human race. When God loses faith in humankind, he sends his legion of angels to bring on the Apocalypse. Humanity's only hope lies in a group of strangers trapped in a desert diner with the Archangel Michael. No wonder the ice cream man shown here (right) seems to have more on his mind than a lemon popsicle.

Doug Jones: *Legion*, 2010
Director: Scott Stewart, Bold Films

" *Death has become a middle-class business. There's no future in it.* "

Joyboy's mother likes her food, but her diet is far from ideal. It cannot end happily. Based on Evelyn Waugh's biting satire on both the film and the funeral industry in the USA, Christopher Isherwood and Terry Southern wrote the screenplay, making this a cutting edge movie of the 1960s. Not all the Hollywood old guard appreciated the joke.

Ayleen Gibbons: *The Loved One*, 1965
Director: Tony Richardson, MGM

Actress, orange seller and mistress to Charles II, Nell Gwyn was never accepted in royal circles, although like so many monarchs before and since, Charles vastly preferred her company. In this picture, they are enjoying an intimate dinner, with enough food to feed both Drury Lane and the entire royal court.

Anna Neagle, Cedric Hardwicke: *Nell Gwyn*, 1934
Director: Herbert Wilcox, British And Dominions

Greta Garbo (left) starred as Queen Christina of Sweden in this classic movie. Her co-star was real-life lover, John Gilbert. Their sizzling off-screen romance thrilled and shocked audiences in equal measure. Queen Christina was involved in an abdication debacle when she had to choose between her Spanish lover and her throne. Here, we see her in a rare moment of relaxation, anticipating the simple decision of which luscious grape to eat first.

Greta Garbo: *Queen Christina*, 1933
Director: Rouben Mamoulian, MGM

Charles Laughton (right) made this role his own in 1933, and generations of children carry the image of the portly king, gnawing on a chicken leg and hurling the bones over his shoulder, as their abiding impression of one of history's most famous monarchs. Henry VIII – a man of large appetites.

Charles Laughton: *The Private Life of Henry VIII*, 1933
Director: Alexander Korda, London Films
(ITV Global)

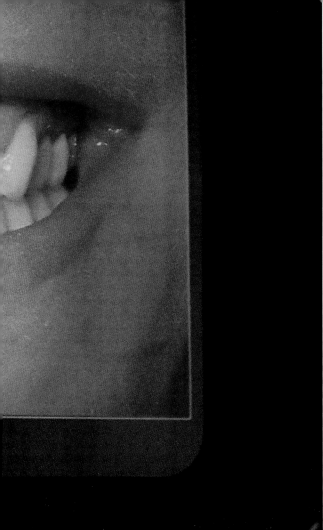

There is nothing like a perfect smile to win friends and influence people, but what is it about dentists and crime? Andy Fiddler is a dentist and salesman who becomes embroiled in a plot of murder, revenge and violent, suspicious undercover agents. Not a lot to smile about there.

Eugene Levy: *The Man*, 2005
Director: Les Mayfield, New Line
Photo: Ava Gerlitz

Former SS dentist, Szell, 'the White Angel' of Auschwitz, is wrapping up loose ends to smuggle priceless diamonds out of the United States. A history graduate is unwittingly caught up in the plot. Attendance at regular dental check ups diminished dramatically when this movie was first screened. The scene of drawn out torture (so slow it is like pulling teeth) of Babe in the dentist's chair is famously one of the most terrifying in cinema history.

Laurence Olivier, Dustin Hoffman: *Marathon Man*, 1976
Director: John Schlesinger, Paramount

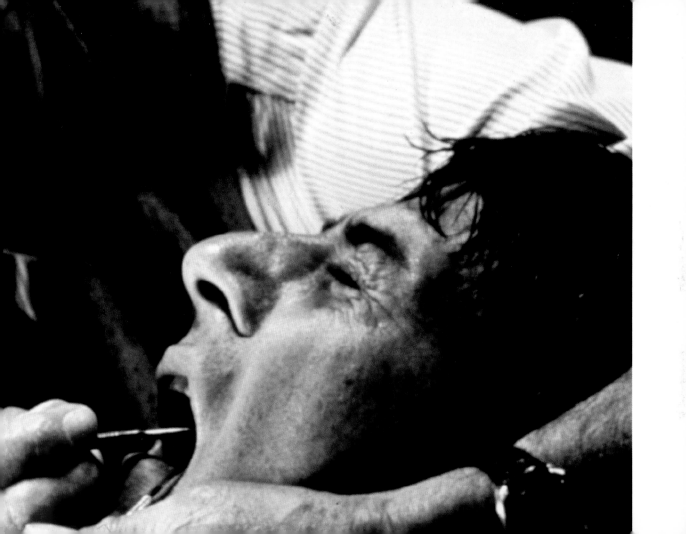

Head of the family of alien observers of life on earth, Beldar experiences the joys of modern dentistry in the process of being 'domesticated'. This comedy satire featured fifteen former members of the cast of the award-winning TV satirical sketch show, *Saturday Night Live*, on which characters from *The Coneheads* made their debut.

Dan Aykroyd: *The Coneheads*, 1993
Director: Steve Barron, Paramount

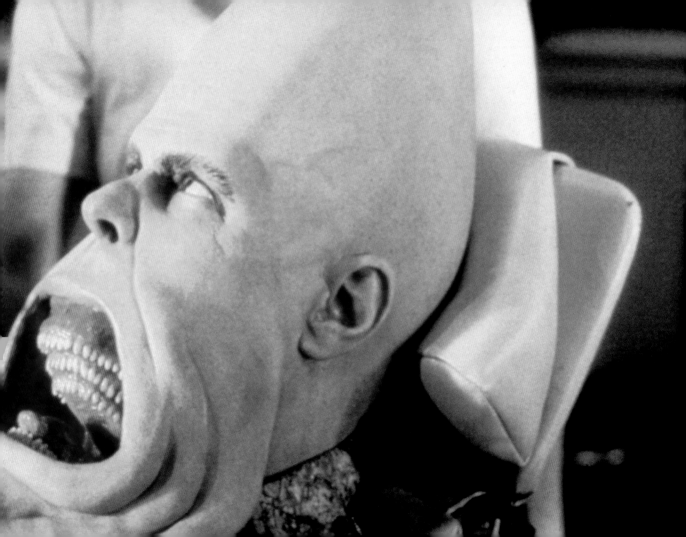

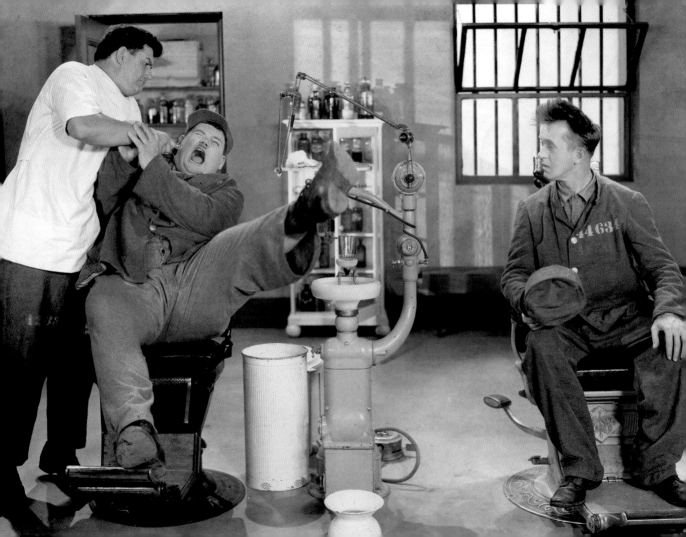

Laurel and Hardy (left) face the gentle ministrations of the prison dentist in this jailbird comedy. Put behind bars during Prohibition, Stan's loose tooth gets him into trouble because it sounds as if he is blowing raspberries. A daring escape leads to the usual mayhem.

Laurel and Hardy, Otto Fries: *Pardon Us*, 1931
Director: James Parrott, Hal Roach/MGM

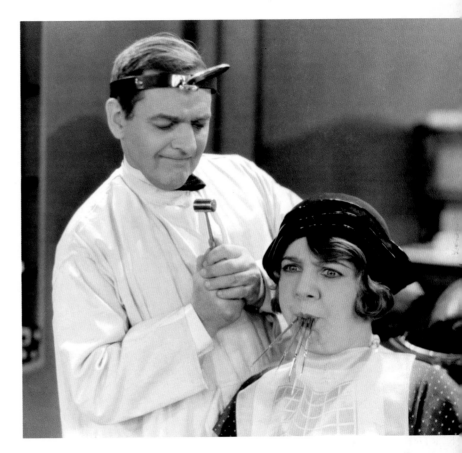

Doctor patient protocol seems to have been neglected when it comes to this husband and wife team (right). Neither seems very happy with the arrangement but the dentist definitely has the upper hand – as always.

Mr. & Mrs. Jack Norworth:
The Naggers At The Dentists, 1931 (?) Vitaphone

'Twas the night before Christmas and all through the house' (left)…Beautifully laid festive table, hours of preparation in the kitchen and eager anticipation of the feast to come – now, who let the dog out, who, who?

Santa Buddies, 2009
Director: Robert Vince, Walt Disney Pictures

Poor Ellie (right), spoilt heiress on the run, is learning hard lessons about life without the good things from Peter Warne, an undercover reporter and soon-to-be love interest. Hardship indeed: fresh, free, organic carrots, just growing by the roadside and Clarke Gable to show you how to munch them.

Clark Gable, Claudette Colbert:
It Happened One Night, 1934
Director: Frank Capra, Columbia

> *How many of you have self-help books?*
> *Okay, that's your first problem.*
> *You can't help yourself, because*
> *your *self* sucks!*

Roger, is hoping that 'life lessons' from Dr P. will give him the confidence to win the girl of his dreams. Teacher and student must share the same dream if success is to be achieved. However, Dr P. would also like to win the girl of Roger's dreams, and therein lies the difficulty. Lesson one: live lobsters can mean nasty nips.

Jon Heder: *School For Scoundrels*, 2006
Director: Todd Phillips, Weinstein Co.

When these girls fight dirty, they fight dirty! Though it is interesting to note that despite 'no holds barred', the biter shown here still has the presence of mind to display her legs demurely, but to maximum advantage. Still it is good to have a role that she can really get her teeth into. Bond at its best.

Martine Beswick, Alizia Gur: *From Russia with Love*, 1963
Director: Terence Young, Danjaq/EON/UA

It is a truth universally acknowledged that this is the most terrifying thriller ever made and that Anthony Hopkins' portrayal of cannibal serial killer Hannibal Lecter has never been surpassed. As something of a gourmet he famously enjoyed Chianti and fava beans…

Anthony Hopkins: The *Silence of the Lambs*, 1991
Director: Jonathan Demme, Orion
Photo: Ken Regan

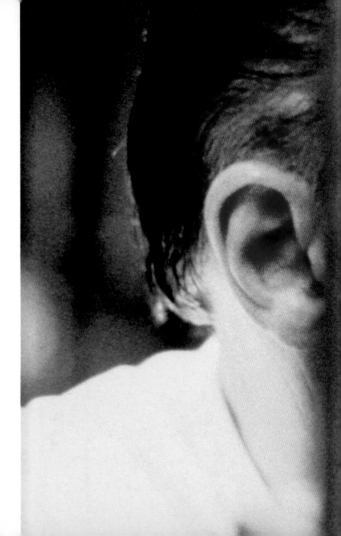

The use of Jaws' metal teeth as well as his huge hands as weapons with which to menace James Bond in *The Spy Who Loved Me* was a devilishly clever masterstroke. Fortunately 007 seems to have the measure of the man. At over seven foot, this is no mean feat. The metal teeth were extremely uncomfortable and Kiel could only wear them for about two minutes at a time during filming. In order to simulate the character's metal teeth, Richard Kiel's stunt double, Martin Grace, used pieces of orange peel wrapped in tin foil.

Richard Kiel, Roger Moore:
The Spy Who Loved Me, 1977
Director: Lewis Gilbert, Danjaq/EON/UA

In a typically macho role for Anthony Quinn, he plays
Zampano, a travelling showman who exhibits feats of strength
in village squares. His act is to break a chain wrapped around his
chest. He hands around a hat for money and then moves on to
the next town. Here, in a display of bravado, he bites the chain.
That can't be good for his teeth.

Anthony Quinn: La Strada, 1954
Director: Federico Fellini, Ponti-De Laurentiis

Is this the archetypal temptation? Young
and lovely Cora Ryan helps inspire an
ageing artist, played by James Mason,
when he retreats to an offshore island
in search of his muse. Interestingly, in
a classic case of life imitating art, James
Mason met his future wife, Clarissa
Kaye, on the set of *Age of Consent.*
History does not relate whether there
was any fruit involved.

Helen Mirren: *Age of Consent*, 1968
Director: Michael Powell, Nautilus Productions